# Best Valentine Book

### ABC Adventures

Written by Pat Whitehead

Illustrated by Paul Harvey

**Troll Associates**

*Library of Congress Cataloging in Publication Data*

Whitehead, Patricia.
    Best Valentine book.

    (ABC adventures)
    Summary: While Big Benny feels blue at not receiving
any valentines, the reader is introduced to the letters
of the alphabet.
    1. Children's stories, American. [1. Valentine's
Day—Fiction.   2. Alphabet]   I. Harvey, Paul,
1926-      ill.   II. Title.   III. Series: Whitehead,
Patricia.   ABC adventures.
PZ7.W5852Bj    1985      [E]       84-8829
ISBN 0-8167-0369-8 (lib. bdg.)
ISBN 0-8167-0370-1 (pbk.)

Valentine's Day is here, and everyone is happy...

# Aa

almost

. . . well, almost everyone.

# Bb

blue

Big Benny is not happy.   He is not happy at all.
Big Benny is feeling blue.

# Cc

card

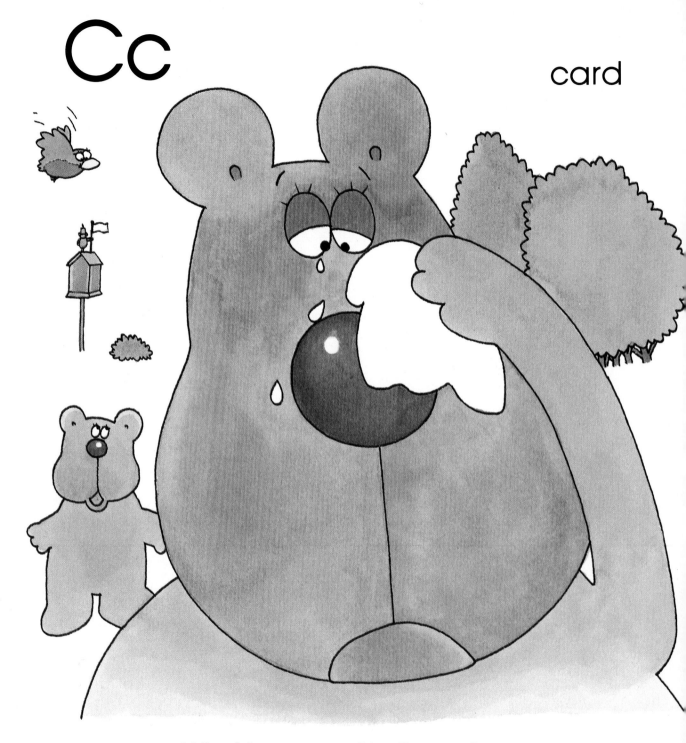

What is wrong, Big Benny?
No card from your valentine?

# Dd

declares

"No cards at all," declares Big Benny.

# Ee

even

"Not even one."

# Ff

fancy

Fay has a fancy valentine.

# Gg

great

Gus has a great big valentine.

# Hh

heart

And Helga has a beautiful red heart.
But there are no valentines for Big Benny . . .
not even one.

# Ii

inside

Big Benny peeks inside his mailbox.

# Jj

jiggles

He jiggles it back and forth.

# Kk

key

He turns the key and opens the door . . .

# Ll

looks

. . . and looks and looks some more.

# Mm

many

How many valentine cards for Big Benny?

# Nn

There are none at all—not even one!

# Oo

outside

TO
BIG
BENNY

But look outside. Oh . . . my.
What's that?

# Pp

package

A package! There's a great big
package for Big Benny!

# Qq

quickly

Go quickly, Big Benny. See what it is.

# Rr

rips

Big Benny rips the paper.

# Ss

string

He snaps the string . . .

# Tt

tape

and pulls off the tape.

# Uu

unties

He unties the ribbon . . .

# Vv

voice

"Oh, boy!" cries Big Benny in a happy voice.

# Ww

woof

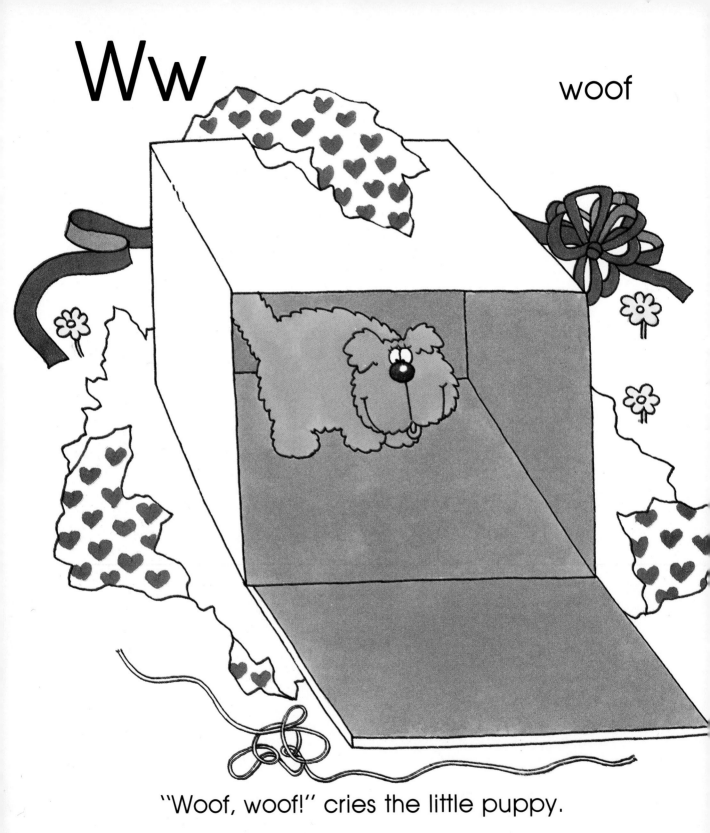

"Woof, woof!" cries the little puppy.

# Xx

exactly

"He is exactly what I wanted!" says Big Benny.

# Yy

you

Happy Valentine's Day to you, Big Benny!

# Zz

Zero

How many valentine cards for Big Benny?
Zero. Not even one.

But Big Benny has something wonderful.
Happy Valentine's Day!